DEAR DAD

Space for Personalized Message

Dear Dad: A Poem of Appreciation

POETRY TEEN SERIES

By Macarena Luz Bianchi

Designed by María Paula Gabela

 To receive a free ebook, exclusive content, more wonder, wellness, and wisdom, sign up for her *Lighthearted Living* e-newsletter at MacarenaLuzB.com and check out her other poems of self-expression, books, and projects.

ISBN: Hardcover: 978-1-954489-56-1 I Softcover: 978-1-954489-55-4

Imprint

Spark Social, Inc. Miami, FL, USA, SparkSocialPress.com

Ordering Information: Licensing, custom books, and special discounts are available on quantity purchases. For details, contact the publisher at info@sparksocialpress.com.

DEAR DAD

A POEM OF APPRECIATION

POETRY TEEN SERIES

Macarena Luz Bianchi

Designed by María Paula Gabela

Imprint
Spark Social Press

DEFINITIONS

poetry & poem

pō′ĭ-trē & pō′əm

nouns

A written set of words that convey ideas and emotions with vivid imagery and/or rhythmic sound.

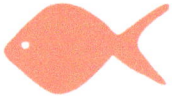

DEDICATION

Dear Reader,

Thanks for taking on the adventure of fatherhood.
What you provide is priceless; through it all, you are always
loved and appreciated.

Enjoy,

MACARENA LUZ BIANCHI

Dear Dad,

You are the ship's captain that I aspire to be.

You show me how to navigate even the most turbulent seas.

I appreciate your love,
encouragement, and
constant belief.

Thanks to you,
I can read a map and will find my
way no matter what life brings.

Your leadership inspires me
in so many ways.
I'm open to adventures each day.

You expand my horizons,
which I love so much, even when you
call me out during our tough talks.

I've seen what is possible with purpose, passion, and perseverance, so work and effort don't scare me.

Thanks to the respect and kindness you show others, I'm not afraid of strangers or what's waiting on distant shores.

Dear Dad,
You are more than a captain.
You are also like the sea.

You can be calm and powerfully
strong when you have to be.

You inspire abundance, achievement, and infinite possibilities when you share your depth, and we remember the ocean is full of fish.

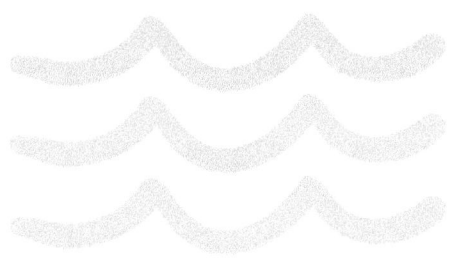

I'm like a surfer riding your waves—of support— while you teach me to trust, enjoy the ride, and go with the flow.

I appreciate the wonder, wellness, and wisdom you instill in me.

You teach me how to navigate through life with freedom and ease.

Dear Dad,
I will always cherish you as I
sail my chosen seas and become
the captain you taught me to be!

DEAR DAD

A POEM OF APPRECIATION

Dear Dad, you are the ship's captain that I aspire to be. You show me how to navigate even the most turbulent seas.

I appreciate your love, encouragement, and constant belief.

Thanks to you, I can read a map and will find my way no matter what life brings.

Your leadership inspires me in so many ways. I'm open to adventures each day.

You expand my horizons, which I love so much, even when you call me out during our tough talks.

I've seen what is possible with purpose, passion, and perseverance, so work and effort don't scare me.

Thanks to the respect and kindness you show others, I'm not afraid of strangers or what's waiting on distant shores.

Dear Dad, you are more than a captain. You are also like the sea.

You can be calm and powerfully strong when you have to be.

You inspire abundance, achievement, and infinite possibilities when you share your depth, and we remember the ocean is full of fish.

I'm like a surfer riding your waves—of support—while you teach me to trust, enjoy the ride, and go with the flow.

I appreciate the wonder, wellness, and wisdom you instill in me. You teach me how to navigate through life with freedom and ease.

Dear Dad, I will always cherish you as I sail my chosen seas and become the captain you taught me to be! ☀

Thank you, Dear Reader!

GET INSPIRED & STAY CONNECTED

To receive a free ebook, exclusive content, more wonder, wellness, and wisdom, sign up for her Lighthearted Living e-newsletter at MacarenaLuzB.com and check out her other poems of self-expression, books, and projects. ✨

YOUR FEEDBACK IS APPRECIATED

If you like this book, please review it to help others discover it. If you have any other feedback, please let us know at info@macarenaluzb.com or via the contact page at MacarenaLuzB.com. We would love to hear from you and know which topics you want in the next books. 🌻

About the Author

Macarena Luz Bianchi has a lighthearted and empowering approach and is affectionally considered a Fairy Godmother by her readers. Beyond her collection of gift books and poems, she writes screenplays, fiction, and non-fiction for adults and children. She loves tea, flowers, and travel.

Subscribe to her Lighthearted Living newsletter for a free ebook and exclusive content at MacarenaLuzB.com and follow her on social media. 💖

Other Titles

BY MACARENA LUZ BIANCHI

- *Be My Valentine: A Poem of Friendship*
- *Congratulations: A Poem of Triumph*
- *Encouragement: A Poem of Success*
- *Friendship: A Poem of Appreciation*
- *Graduation: A Poem of Congratulation*
- *Gratitude is: A Poem of Empowerment*
- *Glorious Mom: A Poem of Appreciation*
- *Happy Birthday: A Poem of Celebration*
- *Sympathy: A Poem of Solace*